curious?about

NETFLIX

BY RACHEL GRACK

AMICUS LEARNING

What are you

2023
NO POSTAGE NECESSARY IF MAILED IN THE UNITED STATES
PERMIT REPLY MAIL
FIRST-CLASS MAIL PERMIT PAID BY NETFLIX
POSTAGE HAS BEEN PREPAID BY ADDRESSEE
Nearest Netflix Shipping Facility
PO Box 4658
Trenton NJ 08650-4658

curious about?

Curious About is published by
Amicus Learning, an imprint of Amicus
P.O. Box 227, Mankato, MN 56002
www.amicuspublishing.us

Editors: Ana Brauer and Grace Cain
Series Designer: Kathleen Petelinsek
Book Designer and Photo Researcher: Sara Hood

Library of Congress Cataloging-in-Publication Data
Names: Koestler-Grack, Rachel A., 1973–author.
Title: Curious about Netflix / by Rachel Grack.
Description: Mankato, MN : Amicus Learning, an imprint of Amicus, [2026] | Series: Curious about favorite brands | Includes bibliographical references and index. | Audience term: Children | Audience: Ages 6–9 | Audience: Grades 2–3 | Summary: "When did Netflix become a streaming service? Spark elementary readers' curiosity about the entertainment brand's history, original movies and TV shows, and cultural impact with insightful questions and well-researched answers. Includes table of contents, glossary, further resources, and index"—Provided by publisher.
Identifiers: LCCN 2024050046 (print) | LCCN 2024050047 (ebook) | ISBN 9798892005128 (library binding) | ISBN 9798892005661 (paperback) | ISBN 9798892006200 (ebook)
Subjects: LCSH: Netflix (Firm)—Juvenile literature. | Streaming video—Juvenile literature. | Application software—Juvenile literature.
Classification: LCC HD9697.V544 N4845 2026 (print) | LCC HD9697.V544 (ebook) | DDC 384.55/506573—dc23/eng/20241223
LC record available at https://lccn.loc.gov/2024050046
LC ebook record available at https://lccn.loc.gov/2024050047

Photo Credits: Alamy Stock Photo/American Pictorial Collection, 18, BFA, 14 (bottom), dpa picture alliance, 6, FlixPix, 15 (top), Lifestyle pictures, 2, 15 (bottom), Pictorial Press, 14 (top); Getty Images/AJ_Watt, 11 (top), FG Trade, 13, Jupiterimages, 8, somethingway, 11 (bottom), Victor J. Blue/Bloomberg, 8; Netflix/unknown, 5, 12, 17; Shutterstock/Diego Thomazini, cover, 1, Here Now, 2, 7, 8, Ink Drop, 3, 20–21, Jolanda Aalbers, 9, karen roach, 8, patat, 4–5, Soho A Studio, cover, 1; The Noun Project/Adrien Coquet, 19, arista septiana dewi, 22, Claire Moody, 19, Davindraaja, 19, erifqizeicon, 23, Luiz Carvalho, 19, naomi argi, 22, SBTS, 23

Printed in India

CHAPTER ONE

Is Netflix the top streaming service?

Netflix has many family-friendly shows and movies to watch.

Yes! More than 280 million people have an account. Netflix **streams** all sorts of entertainment **on demand**. People can watch shows and movies anytime and anywhere. All they need is a subscription.

When did Netflix start?

Reed Hastings came up with the idea for Netflix in 1997.

In 1997. Back then, people rented **DVDs** from a store. They returned the movies a day or two later. Reed Hastings once paid a $40 late fee at a movie store. This inspired him to start Netflix, an online movie store. His friend Marc Randolph helped build the site.

Netflix sent out its first DVD in March 1998. It was *Beetlejuice.*

DID YOU KNOW?
Netflix mailed its DVDs in red envelopes. The color showed that something exciting was inside.

How did it work?

People paid a monthly fee. They picked out movies to watch. They could rent three at a time. Netflix mailed the DVDs right to their doors. People sent them back after watching them. Netflix shipped out the next movie on their list as soon as a DVD was returned.

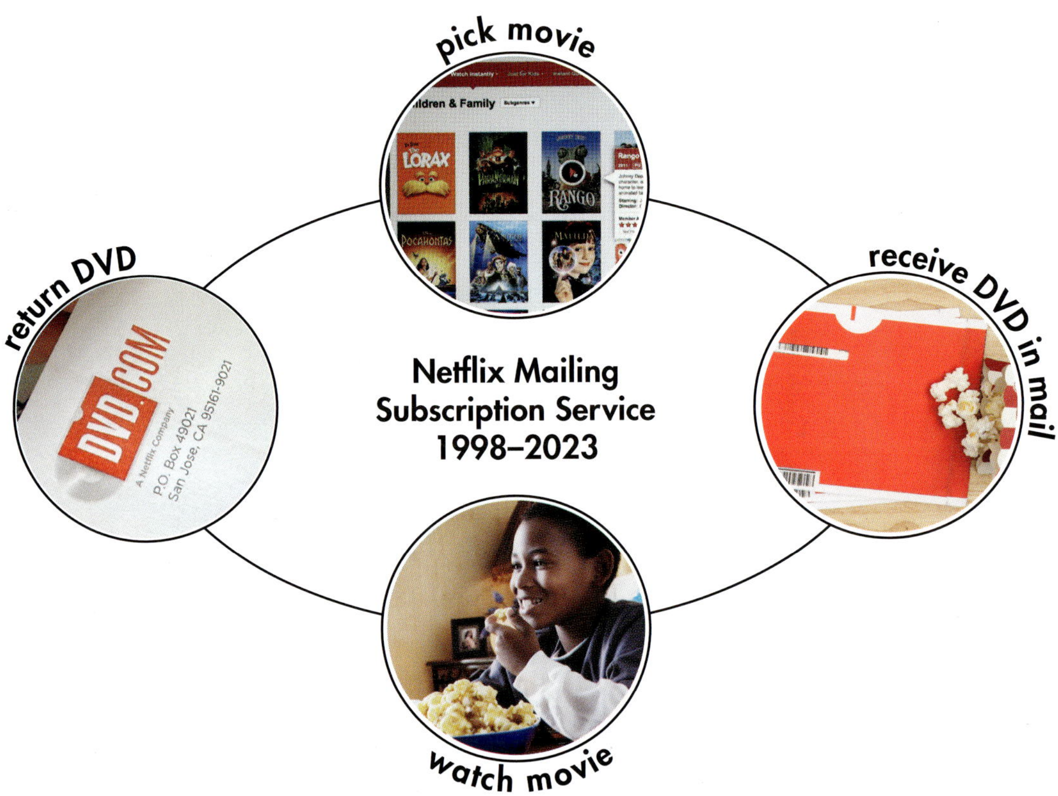

DID YOU KNOW?

Netflix's mail service got rid of late fees. Users just needed to send back the DVD they had to get a new one.

Netflix sent out more than 5 billion DVDs over 25 years.

CHAPTER TWO

How does Netflix work today?

You can stream to almost any **smart device**. You just need Wi-Fi. Watch at home on a computer or smart TV. Use tablets or smartphones on the go. You can even use video game systems. Many devices come with the Netflix app. Otherwise, you can **download** it.

You can watch Netflix anywhere.

Netflix began streaming in 2007. It mailed its last DVD in September 2023.

What can I watch?

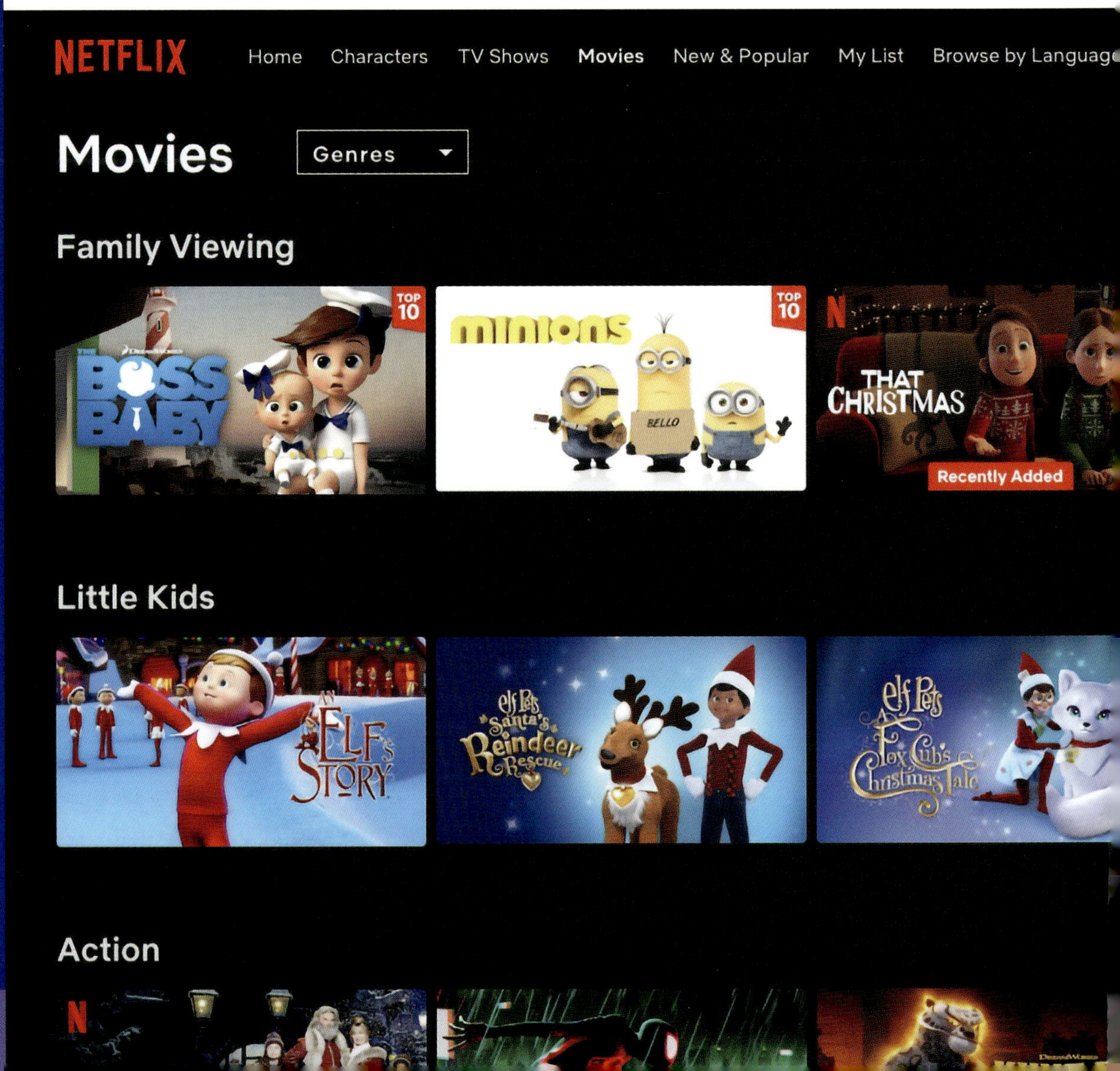

Almost anything. Netflix offers hundreds of movies and TV shows. It has cartoons and music concerts. It also puts out original content. These are programs made by Netflix. The main menu makes searching easy. Just look for something to watch!

Netflix's saying is "See what's next!" There is always something exciting to watch.

DID YOU KNOW?

Most TV **networks** make viewers wait a week to see the next **episode**. Netflix releases full seasons at once.

The Mitchells vs. the Machines (2021)

What original content is there?

The Sea Beast (2022)

Wednesday (2022–)

There are TV shows, movies, and specials. Netflix offers more than 3,600 original titles. The first original show was the adult show *House of Cards* in 2012. Netflix programs are creative. Some have surprising storylines. They are wildly popular with viewers. Netflix originals have won many awards.

Stranger Things (2016–2025)

Why is my menu mostly mystery shows?

Netflix keeps track of what you watch. Maybe you often pick mysteries. Your menu suggests other things you might like. Some viewers find these lists too boring. They want a mix of choices. Want to watch something totally different? Try a hidden menu.

OPENING A HIDDEN MENU

GO TO...

Netflix-Codes.com

Search the lists on Netflix-codes.com. Enter the code into a browser to unlock the menu.

For "Movies Based on Children's Books", type: https://netflix.com/browse/genre/10056

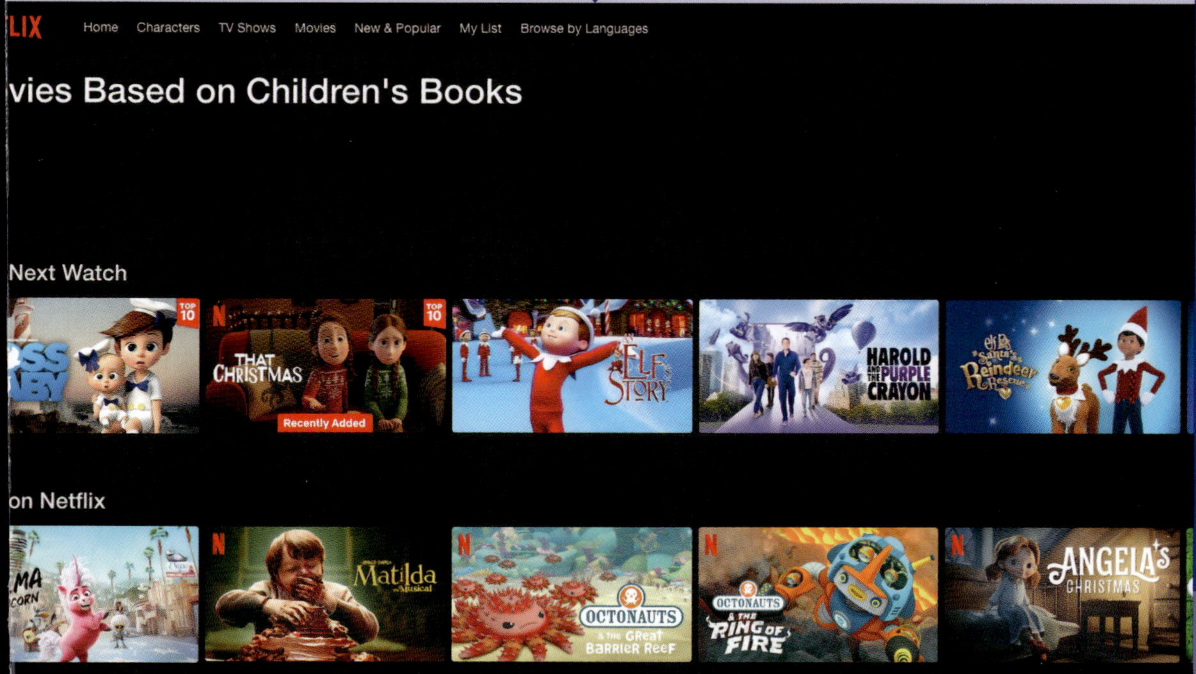

Could I star in a Netflix show?

Netflix helped make Finn Wolfhard and Millie Bobby Brown famous.

Maybe! Netflix likes to cast new faces. This is how Millie Bobby Brown became famous. She starred as Eleven in the show *Stranger Things*. Her fellow cast member Finn Wolfhard also got his start this way. You could be the next breakout star!

NETFLIX BREAKOUT STARS

Jenna Ortega—*Wednesday*

Jacob Elordi—*The Kissing Booth*

Aidan Gallagher—*The Umbrella Academy*

Anna Cathcart—*XO, Kitty*

Walker Scobell—*The Adam Project*

Will I run out of things to watch?

That's not likely. Netflix has more than 18,000 choices. And it adds more every month. Its huge library of original shows keeps growing. Live stream programs pack plenty of surprises. There will always be something new to watch. See what's next!

NO WI-FI? NO PROBLEM!
Netflix lets you download shows and movies to watch later.

STAY CURIOUS!

ASK MORE QUESTIONS

How can I find what's new on Netflix?

What are the hottest shows on Netflix now?

Try a BIG QUESTION: What is dangerous about binge-watching?

SEARCH FOR ANSWERS

Search the library catalog or the Internet.
A librarian, teacher, or parent can help you.

Using Keywords
Find the looking glass.

Keywords are the most important words in your question.

If you want to know about:

- new content on Netflix, type: NEW ON NETFLIX
- the most watched shows on Netflix, type: TOP SHOWS ON NETFLIX

LEARN MORE

FIND GOOD SOURCES

Here are some good, safe sources you can use in your research.
Your librarian can help you find more.

Books

Millie Bobby Brown
by Martha London, 2020.

Television: Then and Now
by Jessica Rusick, 2023.

Internet Sites

Kiddle: Netflix Facts for Kids
https://kids.kiddle.co/Netflix
Kiddle is an online encyclopedia for kids.

Netflix Family
https://www.netflixfamily.com/
Netflix Family is an interactive site with printable activities, games, crafts, recipes, and links to videos for kids of all ages.

Every effort has been made to ensure that these websites are appropriate for children. However, because of the nature of the Internet, it is impossible to guarantee that these sites will remain active indefinitely or that their contents will not be altered.

SHARE AND TAKE ACTION

Talk about streaming with a friend.
Make a list of pros and cons.

Write a script for an original show.
Act it out with friends.

Make a secret menu: Think of a title.
Pick TV shows and movies that fit with your theme.

GLOSSARY

download A computer file that is sent from one device to another.

DVD Short for digital video disc; movies get recorded on DVDs.

episode A part of a television show that is broadcast separately as part of a longer series.

network A group of television stations, such as ABC, NBC, and CBS.

on demand Available whenever wanted.

smart device A piece of electronic equipment that uses the internet.

stream A continuous flow of data sent to a computer over the internet.

INDEX

About the Author

Rachel Grack has been editing and writing children's books since 1999. She lives on a small ranch in southern Arizona. As a lover of stories, Disney is close to her heart. She also enjoys watching her grandchildren play Pokémon games on her Nintendo 64 console.